Procrastinational Coloring Book

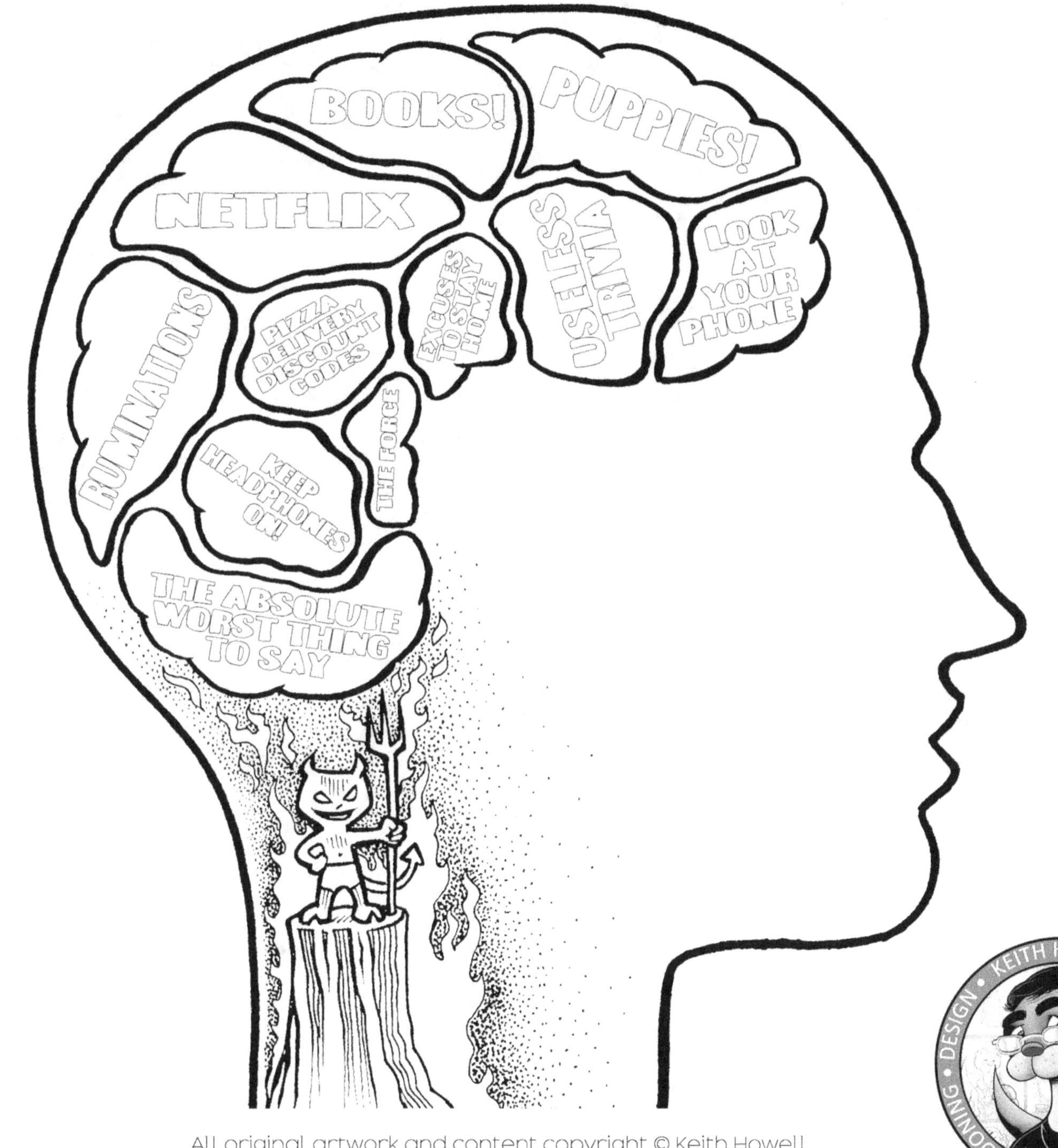

WATCH OUT
WORLD,
HERE I COME!
NO I DON'T.

JUST SAY
NO
TO PARTIES

SAY
YOU MAY
I'M A DREAMER
BUT I'M NOT
THE ONLY ONE
—JOHN LENNON

"I'M NOT LOCKED IN HERE WITH YOU, YOU'RE LOCKED IN HERE WITH ME!"
—RORSHACH

BOOKS
WILL NEVER HURT YOUR
FEELINGS.

EGO
SUM
FORTIOR
SOLUS*
*I AM STRONGER ALONE

JUST DO IT!

I WON'T.

THE TENTH CIRCLE OF HELL
"MINGLE"

"I THINK A LOT, BUT I DON'T SAY MUCH."
—ANNE FRANK

LEAST LIKELY TO ENCOUNTER A ZOMBIE DURING THE APOCALYPSE

Ugh!
Ugh!
Ugh!
Ugh!
Ugh!
Ugh!
Ugh!
Ugh!
Ugh!
Ugh!
Ugh!
Ugh!
Ugh!
Ugh!
Ugh!

I'M NOT
LOST.
I'M WHERE
I WANT
TO BE.

I'M SORRY.
I COULDN'T
HEAR OVER
MY OWN
THINKING.

Cancelling Plans is the Best Plan!
CANCELLED!
CANCELLED!
CANCELLED!
CANCELLED!
CANCELLED!
CANCELLED!
CANCELLED!
CANCELLED!
CANCELLED!
CANCELLED!
CANCELLED!
CANCELLED!

"IN TERMS OF INSTANT RELIEF, CANCELLING PLANS IS LIKE HEROIN."
—JOHN MULANEY

I CAME.
I SAW.
I LEFT EARLY.

GO
AWAY

"CURIOSER AND CURIOSER!" CRIED ALICE.
In this Style 10/6

INTROVERTS
UNITE
SEPARATELY

SOCIALLY
AWKWARD
AVOIDANT

"I thought perhaps she was crazy, but she was only highly intuitive."
—CARL JUNG

Yes,
I'm Awake.
Please Respect
My Privacy
During This
Difficult
Time.

WELCOME TO MY FORTRESS OF SOLITUDE.
NOW LEAVE.

"SILENCE IS BEAUTIFUL, NOT AWKWARD."
—ELLIOT KAY

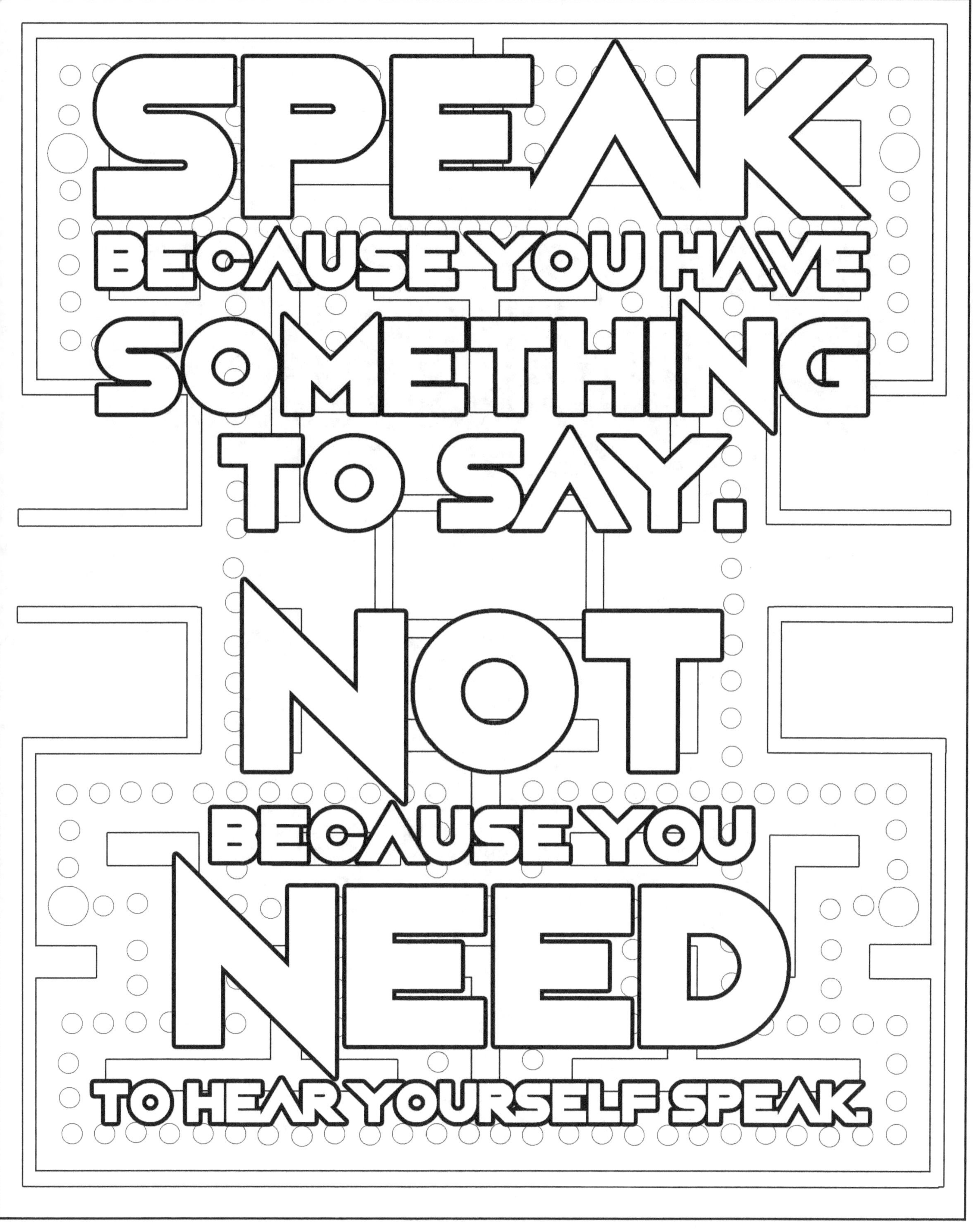

SPEAK
BECAUSE YOU HAVE
SOMETHING
TO SAY.
NOT
BECAUSE YOU
NEED
TO HEAR YOURSELF SPEAK

BEING
ALONE
IS NOT THE SAME AS
BEING
LONELY.

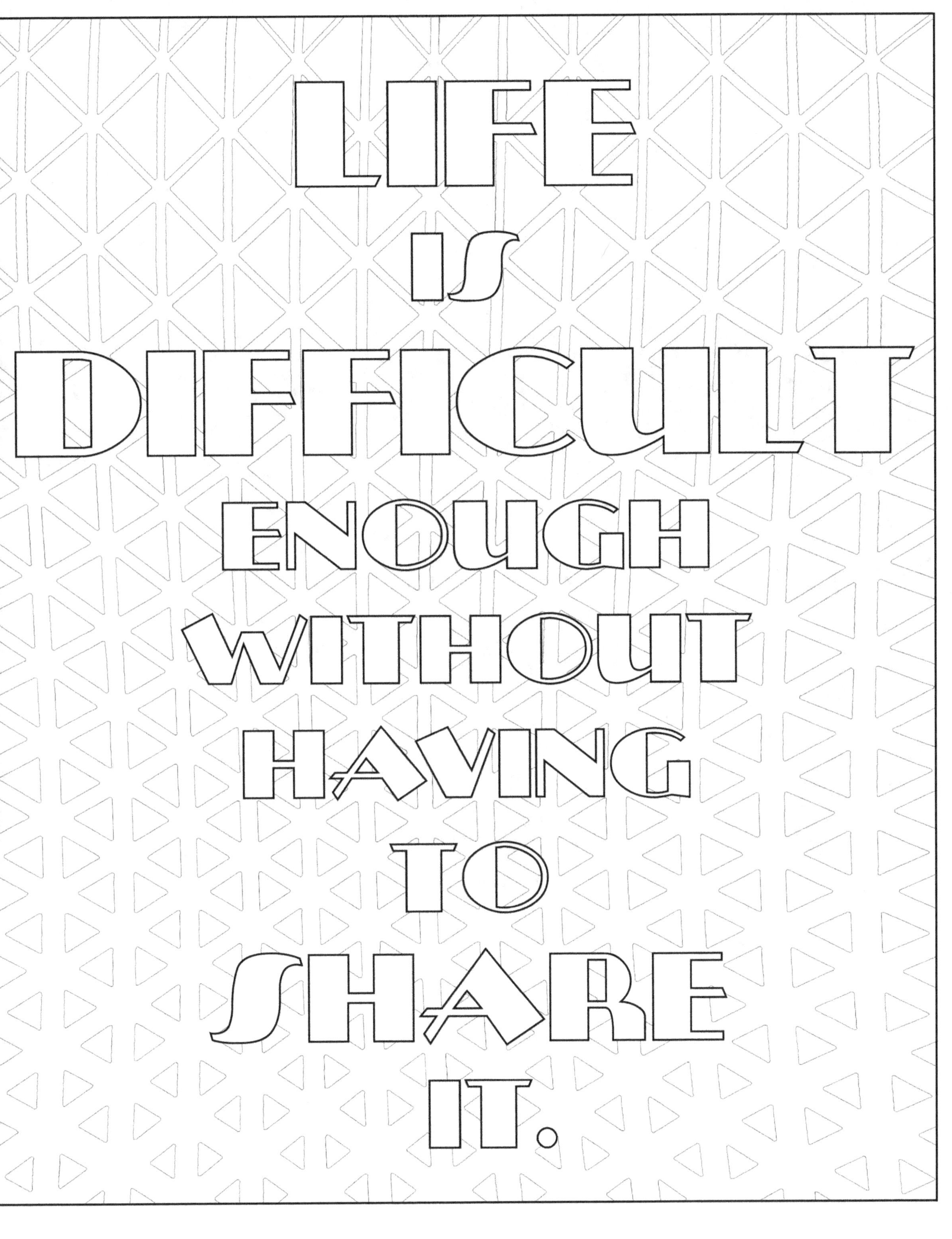

LIFE
IS
DIFFICULT
ENOUGH
WITHOUT
HAVING
TO
SHARE
IT.

PUPPY!

"A BORE IS SOMEONE WHO DEPRIVES YOU OF SOLITUDE WITHOUT PROVIDING YOU WITH COMPANY."
—OSCAR WILDE

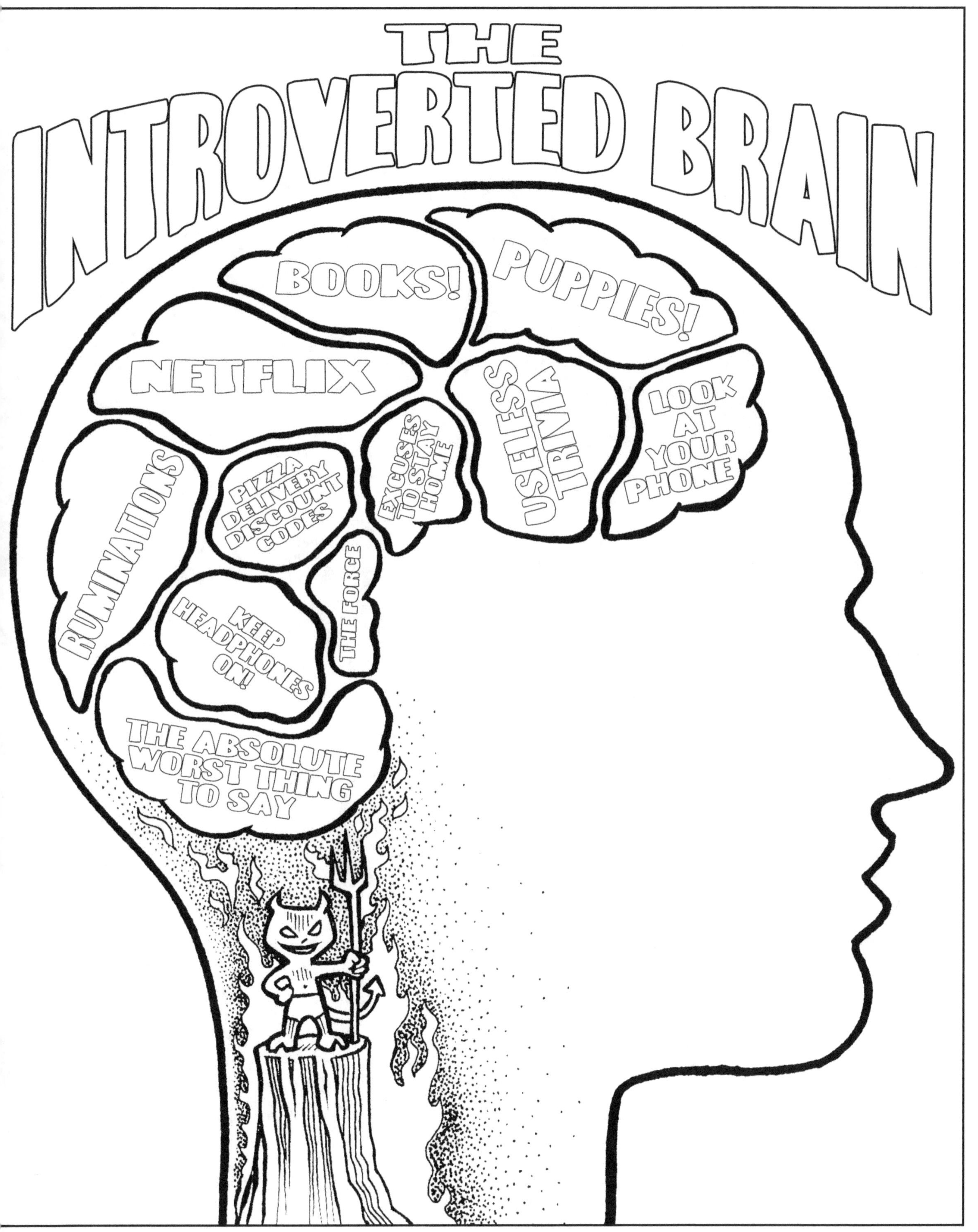

THE INTROVERTED BRAIN
BOOKS!
PUPPIES!
NETFLIX
USELESS TRIVIA
LOOK AT YOUR PHONE
EXCUSES TO STAY HOME
RUMINATIONS
PIZZA DELIVERY DISCOUNT CODES
THE FORCE
KEEP HEADPHONES ON!
THE ABSOLUTE WORST THING TO SAY

Color Me INTROVERTED

ABOUT THIS COLORING BOOK

COLOR ME INTROVERTED! Is a coloring book for all the Introverts out there and for all the Extraverts who wish they were Introverts!

INTROVERT is a Latin term that dates from the mid-17th century that originally meant "to turn one's thoughts inward usually in spiritual contemplation." The term was popularized in the 20th century by psychologist Carl Jung to describe a personality type characterized by reserved and solitary behavior. He further described an Introverted personality as one characterized by an innate orientation towards the subjective and internal world of the mind.

COLOR ME INTROVERTED is a coloring book that is fun for Adults and Young People. It features 30 illustrations uniquely suited to cleverly indulging the hidden thoughts and feelings of Introverts. Each image is designed to fit an 8" x 10" frame space for those who like to display their color work.

ABOUT THE AUTHOR

Keith Howell is an introverted freelance artist and book designer who lives and works in Texas. He has both an art degree and a law degree which means he does not know whether that makes him arecovering lawyer, a starving artist, or both.

His many years of experience in education and educational publishing along with a love of coloring books led to the creation is I THINK, THEREFORE I COLOR educational (*and procrastinational*) coloring book series. This volume is the 5th in the series.

www.profchallenger.com
https://www.facebook.com/artistkeith/
http://www.linkedin.com/in/khowell1
https://amazon.com/author/keithhowell
Instagram and Twitter @profchallenger